The

IMPORTANCE

of PEELING

POTATOES *in*

UKRAINE

The
IMPORTANCE
of PEELING
POTATOES *in*
UKRAINE

———————————

Mark Yakich

PENGUIN POETS

PENGUIN BOOKS
Published by the Penguin Group
Penguin Group (USA) Inc., 375 Hudson Street,
New York, New York 10014, U.S.A.
Penguin Group (Canada), 90 Eglinton Avenue East, Suite 700, Toronto,
Ontario, Canada M4P 2Y3 (a division of Pearson Penguin Canada Inc.)
Penguin Books Ltd, 80 Strand, London WC2R 0RL, England
Penguin Ireland, 25 St Stephen's Green, Dublin 2,
Ireland (a division of Penguin Books Ltd)
Penguin Group (Australia), 250 Camberwell Road, Camberwell, Victoria 3124,
Australia (a division of Pearson Australia Group Pty Ltd)
Penguin Books India Pvt Ltd, 11 Community Centre,
Panchsheel Park, New Delhi – 110 017, India
Penguin Group (NZ), 67 Apollo Drive, Rosedale, North Shore 0632,
New Zealand (a division of Pearson New Zealand Ltd)
Penguin Books (South Africa) (Pty) Ltd, 24 Sturdee Avenue,
Rosebank, Johannesburg 2196, South Africa

Penguin Books Ltd, Registered Offices:
80 Strand, London WC2R 0RL, England

First published in Penguin Books 2008

Page 112 constitutes an extension of this copyright page.

ISBN 978-0-14-311333-1
CIP data available

Set in Minion with Copperplate Gothic
Designed by Elke Sigal

For Owen

Contents

I

II

III

IV

America this is quite serious.

—Allen Ginsberg

The

IMPORTANCE

of **PEELING**

POTATOES *in*

UKRAINE

I

TOURISTS BEWARE

In our free speech they say
There is protest. They say this.
They are wrong. Poetry in America is a hobby

Horse or an earnest earache. Unless it breaks
The rules of syntax and grammar;
Then it simply breaks the rules

Of syntax and grammar. I say this.
I, too, am wrong.
Humorous poetry is published exclusively

One month of the year when everybody is
On summer vacation. More than poetry,
Vacation is protest.

In the Ukrainian town that no longer has an unpronounceable name, the Nazis were putting all the Jews onto trains. Not knowing German, the young woman with one blue eye and one brown went to the Nazi commander and demonstrated with her fist and index finger that she and her elderly mother were very expert in peeling potatoes, and therefore should not be sent away. The commander confessed that his men did prefer their "earth apples" skinned. The next day the young woman with one blue eye and one brown and her elderly mother received permits allowing them to work in the kitchen.

The boy who'd been separated from his sister hid in a sack of potatoes. He told himself: "I am a potato, I am a potato. Potatoes have eyes but no ears. I mustn't move, potatoes don't move. If the Germans come, don't make a sound, potatoes don't speak. But I must breathe on behalf of the potatoes. And if I get hungry, I must eat the hardest one."

The ex-mistress of the SS guard was assigned to the *Kartoffel Haufen*: the heaps of rancid potato discards. She had to sort them to see if anything could be saved. Standing there in winter in the wet potato heap, the ex-mistress of the SS guard would freeze to the ground in her dress. She tried her best to find at least five potatoes a day; for the Nazis had invented this job and the ex-mistress of the SS guard had to show them she was still valuable.

One morning the young woman with one blue eye and one brown found the boy who'd been separated from his sister hiding in the sacks of potatoes. She let out a cry. He was alive but there was nothing for her to do but send the boy who'd been separated from his sister out to the potato heap.

When the ex-mistress of the SS guard found the boy who'd been separated from his sister behind the mound of potato peelings, she wanted to turn him in, knowing that the Nazis would shoot them both. He stuck out his hands and offered a cache of beet peelings he'd discovered in the pile. The ex-mistress of the SS guard took the beet peelings and gave them to the young woman with one blue eye and one brown, who gave them to her elderly mother, who rubbed them on her cheeks and arms so that she would appear healthy.

In return, each day the ex-mistress of the SS guard and the boy who'd been separated from his sister received two small, but fresh, handfuls of potato peelings from which they survived the war.

All these years later, I cannot think of a more beautiful or true story. But the trouble is that it is principally a story, and in telling it I have made both you and me ugly. The actual lives that are lived in atrocious times and distant places can never be told—out of fear that they will be either too beautiful or too true.

If imagination is stronger than knowledge, it is always more to blame.

AFTER THE FLOOD ALL
THE CONDOMS FALL OFF

Anybody can be Noah.
Nobody can be his wife.

Send out the maven, not
The dove. Jump ship and accept

Death. No treasure without
A map. No lap without underlying

Pleasure. Let the mind worry
About the logic. But don't

Forget to drag the body,
As witness, through the sand.

YOUNG UKRAINIANS

"In order to bury a seed, you must eat
Or fuck it," she ate. "Pure factory aesthetic."

"Gimme love, gimme love, gimme the sweet
Unprotected love of laughter," he ate.

"To the living, I have to defend the rights of
The corpse," she ate.

"Your voice
Rises like a winged altar," he ate.

"Expectation, a premise
For change, a fork in the pig," she ate.

The parade begins, the parade ends. "Just what
Did the tracks leave in the snow?" an onlooker ate.

"With the proliferation of guns, drugs,
And genome splicing (bully!)," someone ate.

"I can't wait to meet Virginia and Utah. I can't
Wait for the teddy bears' picnic.

I can't wait to come down
In a slow hail of walnuts," they all ate,

And didn't listen to each other.
They explored the new Prague spring

For decades, and convinced themselves
It was like fucking in Chicago.

PATRIOT ACTS

Don't be embarrassed if you don't get it
Right the first time. The *l* finger

Controls the *o*. In making that reach,
Raise the *j* and *k* fingers slightly

To give the *l* finger greater freedom.
Lift the *f* finger slightly and type

Fold your gold in an old bowling
Ball bag. Hold the *a* finger on the *a*

Key. Make the reach without twisting
The elbow. The letter *m* is controlled

By the *j* finger. Type *Come home move socks*
Mock lick and jerk luck. Type *I can*

Go. I can go for them. I can go. She
Has gone for it. Type *He gave cash*

For it. Joe had the new rod and the net
For her. Type *She won't have to go.*

Type *I can hear him sing.* Type
I am going there I am. Yes. Type

I can do this right. I am going. Type
The ? is the shift of the last key

At the right of the first row. Type
Hold the hands steady as you shift

And make the reach for the ?
Type *These sentences are the work*

That I must write now; I must
Write them with ease and control.

This I can do if I write
Just as I think I can. Type *Go.*

Type *Gone.* Type *You must.*

Appalachian Canticle

Despite the fights, the heroic
Couplet is still Ma and Pa.

The logic of a, b, z. You know

What you want to do, but not
What you're meant to do.

A fisher in a small boat gets wet.

But a head is shod nicely
In a canoe. You have to be pretty

Soft to advocate the hard life.

When the nightingale feels
Like she's cheering up, she thrusts

Her chest against a thorn.

The song rises and the family is
Nuclear again. But who can

Peel bananas with breasts? One

Begins eating breakfast and then
One's cut off by Pa's lips,

A pucker from a drunk respirator:

Oh no, Sis.
Let's just row, row,

Row.

As
Stain
Is to satin,
So too were her panties
To her sense of decorum.
She hated the word *panties*.
She hated her stepmother-in-law-to-be.
She wanted to marry her brother, not her bridegroom.
None of this was of consequence just now.
Because she was having trouble
Explaining why when she
Cried, her vagina
Became
Wet.

SEERSUCKER

To the curator of my father in the next room:
His closet of trousers was custom-made
From Circassian walnut. Inside his
Sweaters and shoes are grease-gray. You'll find
His belt buckles busted (he was growing obese),
And his coat pockets will be lined
With pastry crumbs. Opposite, his smell still
Lingers through his wife's clothing,
Like broken wind. There is probably change
In a thirty-year-old coffee can on the floor.
But if you find his seersucker,
With grass-stained knees and a yellow T-shirt
Shoved into a sleeve, bury him in it.
I want to see him sad one more time.

Before vodka arrived on the scene

& ruined almost everything, we held
A rainproof little newspaper above the dim
Hours, the loaves of black bread. There
Was a contentment with the abridged
Dictionary, the pantyless dresses, the eaves
Of the grand cathedrals yielding. There were
Fair Finns swimming along whittled-out
Horizons. There were unmalleable days
Perched under umbrellas at faux-Parisian
Cafés. There were fleshy winters, gaudy
Falls, bumped-off springs, and summers
Of sponged-down bodies. But now,
The only news we can be certain of
Is that it's been raining, on and off,
Forever. Or as far as Moscow can tell.

Brilliant Pebbles

Ukraine is a country of one official
   millionaire, a song for
   hirsute ladies, a maritime agency
   providing crew.

Ukraine is a *what?*
   Ukraine is being blundered
   by foreign words, as ugly
   as a road diverting

Gas, doing the splits, guilty
   of the Black Sea. Of course
   Ukraine is ready to acknowledge
   its debt, obligated to marry

Belarus, who is humped at her
   shoulders and likes to pinch her ex's
   uranium. Ukraine is about
   how a boy tries

To lose his way of life by accepting
   Europe's birthright. Or how
   a girl in a village in India,
   surrounded by water,

Gives out humanitarian
        blowjobs and banners
        made of two equal, horizontal
        blue and yellow fields. Ukraine

Is that large (the largest) country
        nobody can find on a map;
        the world's #7 arms exporter;
        well-adapted to endure

Cold piss, copyrighted;
        pleased to present America in new
        sanguine flavors. Ukraine
        is preparing for

The Chechnyan vaccination:
        stronger than venison, a nice
        piece of ash, a joy
        to rape, a support group

For youngsters obsessed
        with 19th-century Russian
        poets. Ukraine is safe to sink.
        The nozzle through which

Puke is forced, the towel
      from which it's wrung. And now
      available in your area
      far away from home.

Ukraine is not a nut,
      but you can give it to a monkey.
      Ukraine is that bony little
      saint, looking forward to a future

Of never being felt up.
      Ukraine is the most beautiful winch
      in the English language
      from which to hang yourself.

Pretzels Come to America

Legend has it that Houdini, the son of a rabbi, picked his first lock
Because he wanted a piece of boysenberry pie his mother was keeping

Dead-bolted in the pantry. A busted closet means trouble. Doesn't it
Seem that as soon as you get one thing fixed in the house something else

Falls apart? Say, I might as well punish myself for Mommy's cancer,
Because who else is there at the foot of the bed to discomfit. Bedrooms

Really are nice in all-white. Sheets, curtains, lamps, laser-white metal.
The most important place for a favorite painting is opposite the bed:

The last impression you see at night, the first when you rise. Upstairs
The house has an expiration date, just as Henry James did. Poor Henry

Was criticized for not liking dumb people. He avoided women especially
Because one lady had fallen in love with him and then committed suicide.

They say that before Henry died he thought he was Napoleon. And it
Turned out that he did know a lot about Napoleon, just not the right sorts

Of things that made dying easier. Houdini, James, Napoleon. Neither
Houdini nor James liked to be called by their first names. But Napoleon

Loved his first name so much he destroyed many lives in order to
Keep it popular. Three great men, three great holes. Like in the pretzel.

Medieval monks gave pretzels to children who had memorized their Bible
Verses and prayers. To reinforce a lesson: the three holes in the pretzel

Represent the Christian trinity. Today there are 28 different kinds of
Pretzels in the world and that number continues, in fits and starts, to grow.

Meditation on the
Golden Gate Bridge

All things aspire to weightlessness. —Charles Wright

What tremendous possibilities—the way
    Japanese train passengers have used "stem-and-leaf"
Timetables for decades
    without ever knowing their fancy names—how at the end

Of the day the businesswomen's suit skirts are speckled
    with horse dander
Though they've been traipsing only city streets—and to paint
    black well is simply to put the right brush

Into the left hand, or to reach the popular
    Buddhist belief that if a man becomes a priest, his descendants
Shall be saved for five generations—why
    there's something so precious

About a boy pianist inspired by his pet chickens,
    writing compositions like "Hydrogen Sleeping"
And "Helium Dances to Heaven"—and
    a thirteen-year-old girl who ended her eleven-year vow

Of silence, which began when her mother made her
    get her tonsils removed, with the words "thank you"—how
Young the man is, that wetback standing
    on the corner, who measures days in pecks of strawberries—and

Then suddenly out come I, riding
      syntax and grammar like a broom plunging
An asshole, who so often wishes to cut the body loose—for
      if it must be

A pure *Yes* or *No* as to whether weightlessness is
      the way to happiness, then *No, Professor Wright,*
Not yet, not until someday
      I jump—

TO STEP IN GOD'S CLOUD

My Father, my Father, what you demand—
A sad woman on a summer day.
Root and grape, pear and bean,
Kites and blimps and birds.
Yes it's true, I can arouse strange sighs in
A widower. You have lived too many lives
Keeping Your wishes to Yourself.
I am appearing, yes it's true,
Coming up the ladder
Hair spinning, webbed, lengthening through—

HOLY SONNET

Sometimes the subject matter is hard to pass up.
Take Jesus. He was a very secure artist.
He didn't doubt his talent. He never talked
About it because it was like having blue eyes.

It's now become established fact, however,
That his eyes were a dark chocolate brown
And that he was perhaps a little gay. Mother
Mary herself would mourn such a thing.

No matter what you believe, please recall
The blood of Christ. At the end of the service,
None of it can be left in the goblet. And all
Of us should be drunk. As a professional,

I can spit-taste one hundred wines in an hour.
But if I'm swallowing, I can taste only ten.

Bow Job

I was thinking I like birds,
For instance,

But I don't
Want to touch one.

I like windows,
But I don't want to fall

Or be tossed from one.
And yet I adore the word

Defenestration.

Hope, prosthesis for

Like Nietzsche I hug a horse but it doesn't help
The women still make fun of

The eczema on my penis and it's run-of-the-mill
Stupid of me to line the plank

With suntan lotion who can live without
Self-gratification who can live et cetera

It's hard not to think
In terms of winning and losing and losing

More it's hard it's soft it's hard and then
She says O brother you look

So young just as well
Alive not hung

THE HOLIDAYS

You may have to resort to three-
Hand masturbation or possibly
The ding-a-lings of other men.

Because to sympathize with Father's
Suffering, you'll have to draw
On your own know-how; nothing

Beats a penis like personal
Experience. Therefore, this is a good
Poem if you can relate to it;

It's a civil war if the enemy gets
Hurt and you remain safe; and,
Something is true if it appeals

To the head of the table. These
Are not facetious statements.
That the story of gore gets

Sold is the story. For the old
Music often becomes the new
Hope. All the flooded then poldered

Hymens, all the sequestered
Farts that only defer laughter.
As the number of bombs transcends

The number of babies, men shall
Release their penises into the fields
Of fetching women. For although

We know that Christ was a great
Empathizer, was He not also
One of the thieves who got away?

PLAGIARISM

A few years ago, a company of Indians was captured on the Western Frontier. Among them was a number of stolen children. They had been with savages for years. Word was sent throughout the region, inviting all who had lost children to come and see if among the captives they could recognize their own. A long way off was a woman who had been robbed of her darlings, a boy and a girl. With mingled hope and fear she came. They were strangers to her. She came nearer and, with eyes filled with mother-love and earnestness, peered into their faces, one after another; but there was nothing in any that she could claim. Nor was there anything in her to light up their cold faces. With the dull pain of despair in her heart, she turned away, then paused, choked back the tears, and, in soft tones, began to sing the touching hymn that she had long been wont to sing to her little ones. The first stanza was not completed before a boy and girl ran up to her exclaiming, "Mamma! Mamma!" and she excitedly folded them into her bosom. When they returned home, her husband did not have the heart to tell her that these red-faced children were not her own.

SIDS

It's sad—Mom and Dad
Named him Sydney

Because they didn't think
God would ever be so ironic—

Ask them what they might
Have done differently—

Gotten up that one last time?
Maybe they should've run—

Ask them why these words are
Here—then ask them if

There's a future for irony
Or the spare son—me

II

———————

A Brief History of Patriotism

5000 BCE | It is around this time that the potato is first cultivated by the ancient peoples of the Andes.

476–1000 CE | At some point during the Dark Ages, it is believed that a band of potatoes makes its way across the Bering Strait, but this remains only a hypothesis.

1100–1500 | The Incas grow, eat, and worship the potato, and often bury it with their dead.

1536 | The first European to see a potato is Spanish conquistador Pedro de Cieza de Léon. He promptly conquers it.

1565 | Another Spanish conquistador, christened Padre de las Patatas, takes the potato back to Spain in lieu of the gold he did not find.

1589 | The Italians discover that the potato is part of the nightshade family, related to tobacco and tomatoes. In this same year, a Florentine noblewoman discovers gnocchi between her legs one morning.

1604 | Shakespeare invents mashed potatoes, potato pancakes, twice-baked potatoes, thrice-baked potatoes, and very burnt potatoes.

1605 | In France the potato is outlawed for fear that it causes leprosy, syphilis, and rampant sexuality.

1620–1750	{Here, unfortunately, there is a small, inexplicable lacuna in the research.}
1755	Samuel Johnson includes the word "tater" in his dictionary.
1778	In a war between Prussians and Hapsburgs, neither side is able to win on the battlefield, so both try to starve out the other by stealing and eating the enemy's stockpile of potatoes.
1823	The Belgians invent French fries.
1845	Potato crop failure in Ireland, one million people starve to death. The Irish become famous.
1853	Out of spite for an insolent customer, half–Native American, half–African American chef George Crum invents the potato chip. His creation becomes exceptionally popular, but he forgets to patent it.
1871	The Idaho Potato is invented in Massachusetts.
1899	During the Alaskan Klondike gold rush, miners discover that potatoes are high in vitamin C and are thus worth their weight in gold. A pound of potatoes is traded for a pound of gold.

1926	Ms. Laura Scudder invents the paper bag in which to put potato chips.
1944	Unwilling to take the abuse any longer, Anne Frank writes of her odium of potatoes.
1955	The first baked potato to be microwaved is microwaved by the Raytheon Corporation.
1968	The Canadians invent instant potato spuds.
1971	The International Potato Center (CIP) is established in Lima, Peru, with the mission to help developing nations increase potato production and consumption.
1989	A small group of academics tries to reclaim the potato for itself and begin calling it the "super tuber," but this never really catches on.
1994	Potato consumption is on the rise in most parts of the world. China leads all nations by producing 40 million metric tons, followed by Russia (34 million), Poland (23 million), the United States (21 million), Ukraine (16 million), and India (15 million). Average annual per capita consumption is reported to be highest in certain highland regions of Rwanda (153 kg).

2001	Americans eat 19 percent of their meals in automobiles, and each automobile weighs, on average, 3,900 lbs.
2006	Although the potato becomes a prime candidate for farming in outer space, the results of a nationwide poll suggest that most people believe the potato is too modest to accept.
2008	Still betting on peace after decades of multilingual discourse, the United Nations names this year as the International Year of the Potato (IYP).

Poem for the U.S. Department of Agriculture

At the Annual Luncheon of course I pass up
The orange pom-poms of roe and reach for the BLT.

It's a very formal affair, and looks and tastes
Real but is probably fat-free. Lots of people

Mistake a rock for a bear, but almost no one
Mistakes a bear for a rock. There are strips

And strips of bacon and malls across America.
Scholars say that while he was writing *Lolita*,

Nabokov ate hundreds of "pigs in a blanket."
On The Mall in D.C. people play softball, watch

Fireworks, and occasionally clutch terrible
Placards. What about a replica of the Capitol

In bacon? When I'm very hungry, I think
I could eat one at an all-night, all-bacon diner.

What about a flag of bacon? Oh I would
Not have the courage to fly it. For who would

Apologize to the pigs and hogs and sky?

J. J. AUDUBON

I was born in Saint-Domingue and raised by the Massacre River and
Once on its banks a pack of large boys beat me with wooden spoons
Until I cried and struggling with my internal cosmos suddenly the sky
Appeared bitter-plump but with edible stars and they said
They wanted to look at my tears under a toy microscope

And I still don't know much about those boys whether they had sisters
Who were handsome like painted buntings or mothers
Who wore scoop-necked sweaters in blistering winters
But I discovered why a snail wears a helmet and why
A bird will die of asphyxia if it does not sing

A Few Inches of Dead Flesh

My fingers are weary with writing
As if they haven't had enough.
Roll forth, my song, like Herod's decree—
Yellow blood on the dunes.
Let us bring out the heavy dice,
Even though my hands are
Afraid of puns, hidden beneath my sleeves.
Don't blame them if they've loved
Every day
Reproductions of birds in foul weather.

SUICIDE POEM

for Sarah Hannah (1966–2007)

I found
These words

As a child
And have

Been waiting
All my

Life to have
Someone

To send
Them to;

I've never
Had anyone

But you—
Paper,

Tell the tree
I'm sorry.

Tree, tell
The paper

My story.

Chagall Takes a Prisoner

Morning breaches a flying horse.
All day she hears the noise

Of brushes, refusing to fall in love.
She says, "You're not leaving already?"

He says, "I must, I have to go
Shelter the bride and groom."

Each of her eyes reflects
A small house with a pointed roof.

She says, "Don't you want me?"
He says, "Not unless I break you."

Evening offers a black dandelion
And the paint collects in her heavy mane.

I'll Take "Notable Artists of the 20th Century in Couplets," Please, Alex

$200

"In George's black and white
Photo of me

My arms
Are crossed, left over

Right. A small shadow
Under my chin

Itself casts a shadow
On a wicker chair.

I look straight
At you, lips slightly

Vaulted, keeping a black
Crack unhinged.

My face shows no laugh
Lines, no excess

Freckles, no
Signs of movement.

I am twenty-four.
(I have sixteen more.)

But already
You can see from out

Of the top of
My agatey head

Grows a vertical line
Dividing my black

From my gray
Backgrounds.

And the braided chain
On my left wrist

Is fine, loose,
And probably gold."

$400

   "—as fond as I was of the truth
I think I liked the flesh

   Best and then the Dungeness
Crab I liked the frozen

   Peas too (as color complement) and
The strawberry marzipan but not

The bottomless hearts I liked
The charcoal burnt steaks and even

The fatty parts underside
The melon like the color of the face

Of a corpse and (now that
You think like I want you to)

I like your melancholy
Stage name 'I. M. Other' I have

Often enjoyed a witty-titty play
Almost as much as your arms

Hewn slightly above their ears—"

$600

"In a world marked by artillery,
Money, and fashion

Many a fertilizer
Passes for perfume.

Whether or not you like
My work, I got one thing right:

The best paintings are done
On your hands and knees."

$800

"Most workdays
I went looking

For the empty
Rungs of ladders.

Bones, I mean,
They never failed

To appear
Slightly buttered.

The dumbass, the asshole,
The lapdog—

I shot them all.
People say I lived

For the deathbed,
That I was Hamlet

Minus the ghost,
That I started the rumor

Moses had gotten his
Testicles cut off.

I don't deny
Everything.

But I never took
Photos of real people,

Only the landscapes
They left behind."

$1000

"What can I tell you about drowning—
That I tried it once? Went down like a hand

Smoothing out a felt skirt, again
And again, never breaking the wrinkle.

Afterwards everybody I met was oddly
Qualified to drown. The garbage collector,

The Harvard scholar, the would-be hoodlum,
The giggly girl (my biggest fan) . . . and when

The sun screened my final dream, I found
Myself under a glass-bottom boat

Filled with angels in Speedos. . . .
"But I'm alive," I yelled up to them.

"Would you like a priest?" one of them said.
"What for," I said, "this is only a dream!"

Three mornings after drowning,
The silence was shattered by a tourist

Who was gracefully urinating in the water.
I asked him why it was so comforting.

"Because," he said, "it's only when I pee
In the river that I know it's truly mine."

$1000   Who was Jeff Buckley?
$800   Who was Arthur Fellig (Weegee)?
$600   Who was Jackson Pollock?
$400   Who was Josip Broz Tito?
$200   Who was Frank O'Hara?

47

LENI RIEFENSTAHL

Abhorred. O she was. And how she lived for
More than a century. A darling really
Except for her love of the camera. A woman
No one ever saw crying. Recall how much
Of her there was to go around. Filming
The crowd. How wanted she was. They said
She'd slept with Hitler. The grandstands.
They said she'd slept with Morris, too,
The American who won the decathlon
And later played Tarzan in the movies; he
Ripped open her blouse and kissed her
Breast before 100,000 people. The crowd.
The film. No one dying. Imagine, Hitler's
Voice lived inside her head for seventy years.
The sound of the crowd. An old typewriter
Surfacing. There was no cliff she couldn't
Jump from. And survive. And later no sea
That was not her scene. The crowd. No
One else got off like she did. The film.
To her Jesse Owens was merely four
Gold medals. A few camera flashes.
Seconds. The lathe of the turnstile. The reels
And reels of celluloid she sent to Hamburg.
She only met Owens that once. Not
Wonderful. Not at all. They spent half
An hour debating. She predicted he'd go
Back home and race against horses. And
So he did. She admonished him not

To piss off the Führer. The film of his
Torch. And so what if Owens replaced
That Jewish sprinter in the 400-meter relay;
Owens was supposed to be the man who
Stood in for all minorities, everywhere.
The torch. The camera. The crowd. Leni
Admonished him. And now I you:
Take this book. Finger its edges. Flip
Its pages like the frames of a film. Her torch.
Her sea. Rip apart the binding like that
Delicate blouse she kept in a safe. Prepare
For the prejudice of your own dreams.
That frail body of hers. That furor. That film.
That crowd should have been crying.

ADORNO

As a boy I spent most of my time indoors,
Trapping flies between the curtains
And the windows with nothing
But my flame-blue eyes. Yes, that's me,
On the cover of this stupid book. Isn't
That clever. I first learned about shit
Shoveling on a farm during the War.
Isn't literature a fucking mess? Would
There were a second subject—a pimple or
An epiphany. Hegel divides everything into
Commoners and Heroes. Who are they
Going to arrest—the woman with her
Dress hiked up or the man with his
Pants down? The weight, the culture,
The silence. Unavoidable. Unreliable
Narrators still catch me unawares. Most
People simply want to get through the day.
But not us survivors. Impossible to live
Without an axe to grind. Do I repeat
Myself? Then I beat myself. Such is
The beauty of laying brick. Thick eyebrows
May yet translate into higher sperm
Counts. We're simply unsure. Men don't
Get makeovers. Penny-buttons. Sugar-
Snow in May. Aye, history is the story
Of heroes—give or take their weapons—
But does that alone put hair back
On my chest? Fall in love. Break

Your mother's heart. Understand, I am still
The hero of the story, but I have amnesia.
I can't sing straight. I can't cut a jig. I can't
Draw. But I have a hunch that,
Like a pattern, can be used to make copies
Of itself. Truth is, however, truth isn't
Repeatable. Truth is, my task has to
Do with a diaphanous rope, collateral
Beauty, a sister who never writes back,
And a vulnerary reek of seamen's lace.
Because the mind burdens the past
And the future puzzles the body, this
Story's conclusion shall come to you like
An enemy shot out of season. Like the saddest
Thing I have ever written *My mother and father*
Died in ____, a year I didn't live. Yes,
We must champion our only sun,
For like a pun it destroys as it creates.
And I am so disguised in the clumsiest
Of feelings. Some say this is the con of
Prose. I say, never be content with
The aphorisms of poetry or Auschwitz.

NARCISSISM

for Paul Celan

The man howled against the wall of the farmhouse. The war was no longer
Novel. The sun drew a halo above his head the color of shade.
He took himself out of himself and said,
"One of me will die inside
The other, but which
Other, which
One?"

A Source of Style

Hart Crane vaulted from a ship's railing in purple pajamas.
Purple to soften the blow.

Dear Mr. Whitman,

I picked up a hairy little leaf knowing,
As I did every cranny by heart,
How obscure the woods could get.

I came an awfully long way not simply
To listen to my dolly torque up
A little aspiration for the sun.

I was lost in my thoughts or, more
Properly, I was lost in you, Sir.
When I got back home, I had so many

Chores to do that didn't seem worth
Their names. Now I ask you to help—
Please write me a note from the grave.

Because Daddy still doesn't believe me
When I tell him that I'm afraid
To mow the grass. Always, Sylvia

ROSA PARKS

after Auden after Dante

O what heavenly suffering—
What she can and can't do.
(Save her a dance, Bruegel.)
From knee to shining knee,
Where is the painting of her
Feet, which have never been
Comfortable, arranged in pairs
As peaches are, relaxed, nothing
To do. Where is she not
Not speaking *No!* trying
To keep her world small and
Bold. Where is she confessing
Yes: I am neither arctic ox
Nor Peruvian goat. But ah,
But oh, this is she, nose-flared
And ear-deep along a tangled
Bank, trying to find an end
To the story of people being
Bought and sold. The raw
Years thaw and thaw and
The law makes big men
Amend but a little. When she
Lay down for the last time,
Did You tell her, O Lord—
I couldn't—how white those
Dark woods would get?

ESTIMADA SRA. DEAR ABBY:

En la barbacoa de mi familia el sábado pasado, mi encantadora cuñada y yo teníamos una discusión acalorada sobre su creencia en la reencarnación. Ella quiere volver como una palma o un gringo. Yo intento decidir si me gustaría volver como un pito crestado o el lápiz de labios de ella. A lo mejor esto parece gracioso, pero a mí me pone triste. La cosa más triste de la existencia es el conocimiento de las cosas tristes, es decir, el saber que cuando hayas fallecido y estés muerto ni siquiera sabrás que hayas fallecido y estés muerto. Como si hubiera una diferencia entre fallecido y muerto. No, tampoco es eso. La cosa más triste es que aun si vuelvo a vivir como el lápiz de labios de mi cuñada, no tendría los labios para disfrutarlo. He aquí la trampa existencial del ser. ¿Por qué cree la gente que la reencarnación sería divertida?

Cordialmente,

Sr. Fidel Castro

THE SUPERCOMPUTER FINALLY ANSWERS CHARLES MANSON

I : all the dead bodies you've gotten yourself into
Should : what remains after a pudding or a trifle
Trust : like a trip paid for by a psychiatrist
Green : as an apple on a felled tree
Leaves : the point of having nothing and knowing how to
share it equally
Or : the most frequently occurring word in *Paradise Lost*
The Moment :
Of : a bit of scaffolding pilfered from Patty's nose
Feeling : twilight idol
Thought : the perfect C cup
Without : the bottomless hole in one
Traditional : when the same actor plays Captain Hook
and Mr. Darling
You : every last thing stars

OEDIPUS

for JFK Jr.

You can't stop the clouds
By crashing an airplane.

And without money to protect
Morale, an elegy does nothing

More than inspire middle-
Finger children. Opium, ecstasy,

Star-fuckers. You have to love
Like an ass before your wife

Will fuck you in it. How true
Is true love when you're both

In the dark? Know, the compass
Is more humble than the wing,

Or in your mind the image
Of Father, no-handed,

Doing Mother from behind.

FABLIAU

His beloved was fond
Of eating bullets
In bed, around 2 a.m.

Every night it was
The most evangelical thing he could imagine.
The bullets were

Military-issue, .22 caliber,
Pupil-black, and still a tad uneasy about being
Excused from combat.

She nibbled the bullets
With the care of an orthodontist
And the alacrity of a saint.

One night during her snack,
He turned around and began kissing her
Leg assiduously—

The top, the side,
The middle. He said,
"I've thought about this for a long time now.

Your leg, the left one here . . ."
(He pecked it.) "We're running away together.
It loves me.

And though it's a little
Young, I think I can grow to love it too."
He resumed the kissing,

Deeper. Her mouth
Packed with bullets, his beloved
Began to laugh:

The osculations tickled.
On and on he couldn't stop himself.
Finally she managed to push him away.

But it was too late.
The only thing left was a hole
Where her vagina used to be.

SPELL TO BRING ME
OSAMA BIN LADEN

For a chance to hold
One of his hands, I will expand

A night into a day, a day
Into a kite cornered by clouds.

For a chance to bury my face in his
Pubic beard, I will twist

The length of my own
Hard-won Kalashnikov.

Then I will fight him to the death,
Gently. Yes, I will because . . .

No, it's for him to explain why.
I will sew him a bow tie

And a noose from my daughter's
School uniform skirt.

NIGHTIE, TAKE BACK THE

Over the years I've replaced the dildo in this
Recipe with a frozen stick of

Real butter and when it melts I notice a special
Pinwheel effect in my lover's eyes

Though humans are the lone species
To have face-to-face sex there's nothing

To be ashamed about the truth only lies
In a poem and men are the best

Men can do it's not awful if you're
Pregnant be neither ancient nor a hero

But at times honorable and suicidal
Wince for who else can stomach staples

And nakedness in public praying for
The wicked becomes you and a form of power

III

Green Zone New Orleans

for nine voices in unison

. . .

Forgive me, Home—
I have to go and can't take you with!

They say I can't even take a photo of you.
They say don't bother to burn the master's bed, "We'll provide you a new one."

They say "I'm sorry" isn't what it used to be, but I will keep
Writing your name in the pancake batter.

I will outline your body on our sheets with lipstick.
(Don't get upset if this makes a mess.)

I will no longer cry
Or pretend a wreck is a neat animal.

I will no longer lie—
Most of my thoughts are

Memories and what isn't is a mirror
I break my nose against.

. . .

For I shall leave no
Inheritance but this

Napkin, and thus I have
Come into this napkin

And killed many
Enemies of the State.

Black and pink.
Black and lilac. Black

And scarlet. Black and maize.
Black and orange, a rich

Harmony. Black and white,
A perfect harmony. Black

And brown, a dull harmony.
Black and drab or buff.

Black, white, or yellow
And crimson. Black,

Orange, blue, and scarlet.
Black and chocolate

Brown. Black and shaded
Cardinal. Black and

Cardinal. Black, cardinal,
Blue and old gold.

Black, yellow, bronze,
Blood and sky blue.

. . .

Forecast calls for purpose:
Today there's a difference

Between patriotism and racism.
One puts a varnish on

Barbarism, and the other
Lets barbarians

Varnish the hardwood floors.
Facts first: Jesus was

A gay, black man.
Just say it aloud

And see how nice
It sounds. One reader

Replaces another
Like one leader defeats

One thousand brothers.
Ultimately people are

Meant to be killed.
You can go

To the bookstore
And move all the bibles

To the fiction section.
But what's that

Going to get you?
A backache and your wife's

Mock admiration.
It's far better to ask Christ

To forgive us
These Christians.

. . .

Forgo the heroic
Couplet; there are other ways
To wheedle a ghost. Tears

Are moderately effective—
The sincerity of them doesn't
Matter. Because the depth of

Sorrow can seldom be judged
By a graduated cylinder.
Fasting, too, is

Uncomplicated and tidy
But painstaking
And might take a long

Time. Of all the forms
Of humility none compares
With the soft gel tabs

That can be easily
Procured, gulped, and then
Pumped from one's

Stomach and put back
Into their little bottle,
To be returned later.

· · ·

For autumn is no out. No more harbor
For the master. A pair of nice breasts

In my bed is worth two hundred
Postcards from the French Quarter.

More if I'm reading the Kama Sutra.
What of small scrapes between

People. As in the tale of "The Knife
And the Pea." As in two suicides waiting

To unload. You see, burning down
The enemy's house is actually quite

Easy. You use the laundry line for
A fuse. One grenade through the rear

Window and one match for the cigarette
Afterwards. What gives meaning

To my wife back home? White wine
And shabby suffering. All else is

Only the repeated thought of the cock
In her mouth that's not mine.

• • •

For fun when a woman cries,
We beat each other up.

Then we spend the night moaning.
We pee off the balcony. We

Come in each other's hair.
(The rarest of flowers is not as beautiful,

And come is more natural than hair gel.)
In our world when a man cries,

We call him Mary. For his pride
We eat the baby inside the king

Cake. We exchange clichés for
Oil changes. He says he loves us

Because we dare him to; we dare
Him because he shoves us.

In our world no one leaf can
Feel the sun's reign, and it takes

The whole sky for the termites
To fell the tree properly. If someday

We want to leave this world,
We shall lie down

Still and close
Our eyes until one of us disappears.

• • •

Forget some call love
Bedside grammar:

The body rules
And it's a trick

Of the mind
Not to think so.

You'll never
See your own

Corpse and nobody
Will ever know

Your mind.
God exists to give

Your daughter
Someone to believe in

When you're gone.
On the other

Hand, one day
She will ask

You a question
You don't know

The answer to,
Because the answer is

The question.
Don't act

Nonplussed.
What's the meaning of

Life,
For example,

Is simply a claim
To intelligence

And a pledge
That no other

Hand exists beyond
This one in hers.

. . .

For believe
Me or not,
There are

A finite
Number of
Ideas

And a finite
Number
Of brains.

Those ideas
Compete
For space

In those
Brains.
If faith is

A place
Circumscribed
By the idea

Of its reign,
And I can't
Move your heart

Even with
A bullet
At close range,

Then at least
Press your lips
To this

Page—
The only way
I have left

Of touching
You from
Here.

Forever having calculated our sins poorly
Spent, we see God's last kiss
And raise Him a first fuck. We know

Little about cultivated thought. We
Believe in polyester and yet
Know that polyester debases the body.

We realize that our list is not new.
However our poof of life is shorter and simpler.
At length comes sunset. At length

Grow the mold and debris, which we filter
Down to these lines. We take the nightclub
And score the heart. We are even

Parts siphon and reservoir.
In case of emergency we can be held
Together. We shall open and float

Away like thousands of diapers from the levees.
We who cast anchor but have no rope.
We who show much leg for too little

Milk money. We who pay
The ransom and give back the rhyme.
We are short on superlatives before we die.

We cry like shit.
For fresh underpants won't come
For another six months. For butchering

Is best left to shepherds.
For our final proof
There is no God: there is one.

Minus the staph infection and the sports metaphor.
Minus the crack journalist standing
Before our epitaph: *What it means to fuck*

New Orleans. Here plot is
The sin the hand hides. Plot is the low
Land inside your breast. Hear us now

Because here you're ours. Together
We'll jump from the back of one
Dark horse to the next.

For once upon a time,
Time. As is is,
Take refuse.

IV

SEPTEMBER 12

The world is all that is just in case of emergency.

Having no good guidebook and feeling
Compelled to listen to everybody else's fucking
Advice, directions, and predictions, suddenly
We had to lie down and make the children

The horizon. As if on our deathbed we
Had to choose whether or not to believe in
The Maker once and for all. Because it said so
Right there in the Koran: *If you turn away from God,*

He will simply replace you with other people.
But we had been taught since childhood that
We were special and irreplaceable.
And it said so right there in the Bible:

Thou shalt love thy neighbor as thyself.
But now we were beside ourselves. For a long time
Afterward we argued. Or at least as far
Back as we can remember. Everything before

That is black in the mind and now white
On this page. But don't be deceived:
Letters aren't grave markers.
Over our fears, which are not many but deep,

We've tried to live the children's lives
Through love, and they've tried to give us
More of their lives by screaming
At each other. This is to be expected

From making the same motion with
Fingers, tiptoeing, if you will, sometimes
Banging bodies with plastic keys.
Were it not for the plastic of life, we

Might all perish in a parish of puns
And morbid thought. But thought once
Thought is no longer elastic. Confused?
God does not clarify; we exist.

Which brings us to a conclusion
Having nothing to do with us: We
Have deliberated long and hard about
Writing an introductory essay to a book

You don't hold in your hands right now,
In which we're disgusted by the problems of art
And children and art and politics
And art and war and art

And anal sex; but in the end, which is not
The conclusion of anything until we pass
Away from the memories of
Our mothers and into the children,

We decided an introduction would be
Tantamount to confessing to a crime
One has yet to commit.
If there are errors, therefore, in the work

Before you—things you don't like
Or things you like but not in word-form
Or things you don't believe are really
Things at all—we blame them on the children

Just as you blame them on us. For we didn't
Plan on writing this book. We didn't
Intend to provoke a lot of bad feelings in
Its reader. We weren't even thinking about

War or fear or safety or courage. We know
That you can get those things elsewhere,
That in other arts, say, at the movies,
You can be moved to small tears or that,

Say, at the symphony you can fall
Asleep gently and unnoticed. After all, what's
A little book of poems going to do
For you? We wrote the following words

Because they made us happy at times,
And at other times they made us sad
And then rhyme like assholes.
Don't think that we had a good time

Writing this. Don't think that we had
A bad time either. We simply had time, and that's
Probably a greater sin. For you
Can plainly see, we are not one.

But we are not two either. *We* is this third thing
Between us: the dildo or the children.
I love you, Wife says to Husband,
Now lock the door.

The children love you, Reader/Reaper,
Because there's no one left to adore.
I love you rhymes with *Let me go,*
Or so say the children of dead heroes.

LAST FLIGHT OUT OF
A STATE OF MIND

We chose this plane because we didn't know
      It would become the subject

Of a poem. To us poetry is ludicrous,
      As if telling a hawk he has talons.

As if telling the totally fucked not to use
      Bad language. We have broken

Wind, and we will break wind all the rest
      Of your days. It is the one

Thing we do that doesn't deserve undue
      Laughter. Should you feel

The oxygen drop, should you hear the crack
      Of the flaps, the rap on

The lavatory door, you may use our dead
      Bodies to float. You may

Scream on our behalf. You may not, however,
      Burst open like petals, then

Jackknives. That is our charge, for
      Now cannot be won backwards.

FIREFIGHTER SONG

Though you taught me
Time would not always be ours,

I was surprised when your death
Arrived, an absurdly large

Clock I felt obliged to
Split in two. One half jumped

Inside the stove and burnt
Memories of you

All the way through.
The surviving half limped

Away into the newly fallen
Snow. I followed its tracks as if

Hunting a fox . . . an odd
Sock . . . a dropped stitch . . .

But no metaphor found me
Bearable. Time is

The shore the sea can never fully
Grasp. And I sink with it

Because my arm won't
Let go of my axe.

FOR A YOUNG MALE POET

Man of my blood and kidney—
I, too, suckled from

A browbeaten nipple
Under a wimple and came

Up short. Fight for the penile
Implants and lactation consultants.

For the heart will continue
To beat with an estimate. Sit and write

Now, in search of the land far
From the breath that named you.

FUNERAL DIRECTION

for Pfc. James Thomson

Dice-rammed river
Of time, this winter ploughed
By breath. The waters
Over bedrock creak—you
Could call them frozen,
Though they don't give
Until the oxygen is gone.

The seasons always
Seem to be a form making
Meaning, a kindled motion.
Time heals nothing but soldiers'
Insomnia. You know
You saw lightning strike once
In your life. But no nut-

Strewn shepherd fell dead.
No dune wound itself up again.
Some bastard-bird simply chimed
In, and death came for you
Like you wanted spring to do.

PATRIOT ACTS

The poets taught me that some people are dirty, some
Fancy, and some write poetry! Then they taught me that

All of us are symbols inhabiting other symbols;
That the consumer consumes the worker and the young

Boy consumes the old man and the nubile girl
Consumes her shampoo! I didn't understand

When the poet used all the exclamation points.
I didn't understand where the lawn went after

The lawnmower finished eating it or where
The subway car slept in the dead of night.

They said, "Witness the cider barrel, the log cabin,
The hickory stick, the palmetto, and all the leaves

Of the great books yellowing." I said, "I can't stand
The smell of the library!" They said, "Can't you

See the power of the flag and the cardinal,
Our state bird?" I didn't know we still had a state

Bird. They said, "When Plato defines a line as
A flowing point, are you going to argue with him?"

I said, "If a line's drawn in the sand, then it'd better
Be attached to a rubber band." "You mean

A slingshot?" "No," I said, "I was thinking about
Mother's old bikini." They said, "We're not

Here to enjoy you." And then one of them moved
For his pen. "Don't do it," I said, "it might explode!"

It was a joke. But then they said, "Don't worry, we'll let
You fuck the heroes when we're done with them."

New Pathways to Peace in the Middle East

Rock, paper, scissors (best of seven)

Two equal but separate bitchslaps

Moon colonies

Viagra

Quakerism

Bono

Killer bees

Solar power

Mercy

Tsunami

Game

UNKNOWN SOLDIER

You shot at them and they caught
You and kept you outdoors. After

They gave your ears to the dogs, you
Couldn't quite hear them hack into

Your left arm. When one of them
Whispered to the other, you sat there

Pretending to be better than them.
You didn't keep a memory of your

Wife's scent under your armpit
Because they'd taken it too. You didn't

Think about her when they trapped
Your penis in your zipper.

All evening you could feel them
Stuffing it back inside, their hard

Hands giving new meaning to
The rosy fingers of dawn. And when

The morning sun put part of you
Back together and the afternoon

Breeze hit your face, you looked
Like a basket of rotting blackberries,

A bad collage, or a terrible hoax,
Until I wrote your obituary.

A Truth Is Subject to Its Title

At the museum that is the African equivalent
Of Auschwitz, the hallways are not lined with

Small mountains of hair of Jewish girls or
Strewn with suitcases stamped Horowitz, Goldstein, et al.

Instead, you find piles of macheted skulls of Tutsi
Boys and one of four survivors (out of 45,000 villagers)

Who can accompany you through the rooms.
And if you like, one of them

Can hold your hand or take your photo
In front of the bones of his mother.

"This," he says, "is my mother."
And then after looking at her

Imploded chest, he says: "Oh no, that's not her.
That would be my cousin. There—"

And he gestures with a rock-throw, "That's my mother."
The boy is so calm and polite, and you wonder

Who taught him to speak the King's English.
Both of you walk over to inspect the skeleton.

"No, no, there," and he gestures again.
You spend the rest of the day looking

For his mother. Eventually you give him
Twenty dollars so that he goes away.

But when you read back over what
You've written and rewritten, no matter

How much you would like his mother
To become your own, she won't—

Not least for money, not more for
Your suspending disbelief.

FOR A SUICIDE BOMBER

If you stare right between your thighs
You will find that one of the many beauties
Of poetry is that you can go from a sedentary
Lump all the way to a lean, self-righteous
Hard-on without touching nostalgia. I
Have seen people exaggerate the flower
Of poetry. For example, it can give you
Longer, more distinguished orgasms; it can
Make you fall in love with your mother;
It can placate crotch odor. I have known men
And women who deliberately crap their own
Pockets and leotards trying to suffer the same
Misery of Buddha, Dante, Dickinson, and Li Po.
It's time to put the big myth about these
Pilots to bed. By definition their crying is
A low-intensity way to burn calories, and their
Tears are a low-down way to get someone
Into the sack. Even so, I have worked with
Many people who felt they were climbing
Everest as they struggled through their first
Twenty-minute crying jag. Remember,
You have thought your whole life about how
Wonderful fame would be. Let your
Hand form a loose fist around my trigger
Point. The rules for success are clear: You
Must never give candy to a dandy; and
You must learn to die, like the Moors
On a Spanish galleon, in five-minute shifts.

THE BATH OF RESISTANCE

It's not in the way of the world or the other way
        around or some variation
On a latent tune. The momentum to punish and be
        punished within the walls of

Peace outstrips even rubbish. Friends and followers
        free from satisfaction, expect
A valence like the hard I machination.
        So to make a dirty bomb, hand out

Affection like circulars, where everything becomes
        the world, even preteens flying high,
Snapping photos of themselves
        about to orgasm, where sheer blood-contact

With nonbody objects is old hat. The new way
        of consciousness borders on fake
Rapture, like an ecoterrorist who beats off to
        more than his fair share of disaster porn.

Embedded

"If it's romance you're looking for," said Auden,
"Go fuck a journalist."

And so like hopeful sailors the teenage soldiers drank
Twenty-year-old scotch out of fragile paper cups.

One of them restarted the ancient argument,
"Of course the club is more crushing."

"But," the other interrupted, "the machete is more natural."
After an hour, they finally agreed that the point is to write

In a form that praises the hand and shames the grenade.
"And yet," said the first one, "biting creates

Two explosions—one inside the mouth and one
In the arm of the man who's grabbed you from behind."

"Sure," said the other, reaching for his notepad, "like a kimono opening—
For one tender second the sword both severs and connects."

 "Oh stop it, you two," said Auden, "and simply fuck me
Before this no longer feels like a crime."

PANOPTICON

Tears
Of India
Are the finest
Of tears. Our tears are
Handpicked and specially wrapped
In unique foil and tissue linings to preserve
Their superb flavors. To ensure you have the best
Quality tears, look for this stamp. And remember after opening
The box: Only you decide the breadth and depth of the passage they cross.

INTERVIEW WITH THE EXECUTIONER

Death by injection, Texas. Mike Murphy, d. May 2, 1999.

"It was likes tryin' to pry opens a padlock with a felt-tips pen."

What was—his vein?

"No, his poem."

What about the pain?

"Well, it's energizin' to have adversaries."

Sorry?

"Imaginary pains, y'know, Sean Penn."

The actor?

"Yeah, this guy cry just like him."

My Initial Dwelling
in Nonexistence

In the absence of a butler, I didn't know where
        the gun fit in. Apparently, my murderer
Fired it in the air when he found our conversation
              monotonous. It sounds

Like a brutal act, but in the anti-world
        guns give life. Proof, he was fond of
Saying, is to die for. And now that
           the physicists are proving him right,

I would prefer not to wake the man
        lying under all the bodies. My world is always
Going up in flames as I am practicing the violin.
           Unfortunately, it is a loaner.

THE BLUEPRINT EFFECT

This modern construct was our sickness:
           lazy peace, cowardly compromise, the whole
Virtuous cleanliness, and the contemporary
                "Yeah" and "Fuck Yeah." This tolerance

And largess of the heart which "forgave" all
           because it "understood" all. This small, jet
Black–haired woman with a feisty smile,
             after paying rent and buying infant

Formula and clean drinking water, often said,
           "Some weeks we only eat beans and beans."
Life like a drive in a country to be pitied.
             Life like Beckett's last walk to the beach

In only his underpants which were pink,
           having been washed with a new red shirt.
Life, this muddy little head knocked in
            against a cement playground.

PATRIOT ACTS

Whoever duct-taped kitty with the C-4 must've
Thought himself a genius. And who wouldn't
Send in an animal to do a mortal's job?
By mortar lake and budding sky, kitty stood there
With birdshit on her head. Shrapnel brushed by
And plastic bags rippled instead of flags. She
Swayed back and forth at the entrance to the hotel.
And then—worthy of a copyeditor's pun—
Catastrophe! A bullet hit the kitten killing her
Instantly, saving many people. But what's left us now—
Dried blood and shifting eyebrows, limp cocks
And lopsided divinity? No. I invite you, Constant
Critic, to stroke this paper as you would've
Her corpse. Don't toss kitty into the recycling
Bin because she didn't complete her mission.

DINNER PARTY

When I apply my manhood like makeup,
Everything is at once promising
And suspect: ten-pound barbells

Next to clipped fingernails;
Corncob vibrator beside bag
Of pretzels; the paint of my keyed

Limousine flecking into
The strobe lights of a police car.
When I visit the National Museum of Art,

Every boy who eyes a Balthus
Nude is orphaned to me.
But not in a Third World way.

Death threats may be flattering;
However, I'm learning to detest whining—
"O life, life, I hate to leave"—

Particularly after a close shave, after sex,
After signing off on a sob . . .
A bombardiering . . .

    . . . excuse me, Madam President,
But you just stare at the lamb.
Don't you like it?

READER/REAPER

You get everything
Backwards.

First my bow
Then my speech.

First my ditch
Then my plow.

Who knows—
Maybe you do

Smile more
Than you speak.

I know you're only
After meaning—

You like to ride
Over a bridge

Without seeing
What supports it.

AN UNTENABLE NOSTALGIA
FOR CHERNOBYL

Unspeakable acts may be our epics, and you
        May die in your sleep. Thus find
Your meaning between the lines
        Of mother's hands:

The best-paved streets of Chernobyl.
        All night long the points
Of view are punished. I, too, wanna be
        Ready for the little black dress

That's all the rage. I look into
        The bathroom mirror at that old baby,
The gaze after my own heart.
        What is it about our experience of

A great book? Like a disposable
        Yarmulke, it causes a question:
What to do when you're done with it?
        They say, if you go far enough away

You'll be on your way back
        Home. To a sacred still. I have to
Confess that in my flight
        Often I'm drinking alone.

But I'm sowing. And I hear my interred
  Relatives cheering. More
And more their memories make
  Mockery of the bookshelf. I stand over

The toilet poised and lustful. Happy as
  I am to enjoy the vanity
And vodka, the drunk don't make
  The rules. No. 1: Live long life.

No. 2: Quiver. I figure in a land blessed
  By compunction, what can't be
Lost again. I ape a dictator, a vial of
  Cyanide, a Geiger counter. I rewitness

The charcoal-burnt orange skin
  Imprisoning the fatty pork steaks. I shoot
Quatrains as if they fly from the trees.
  I say: Go now, Little Book,

Make your way without my world.

Notes

"Tourists Beware" takes its cue from Muriel Rukeyser's "In Our Time." The mention of humorous poetry is a reference to *Poetry* magazine's "Humor Issue," which was renamed "Summer Break" in 2007. The month in question is July/August.

"Proof Text" melds a few narratives from www.savingjews.org, compiled and edited by Anna Poray, and from the archives of Yad Vashem, including an educational unit titled "I Wanted to Fly Like a Butterfly."

"Seersucker" is written after Deborah Digges's "Seersucker Suit," which was first published in *The New Yorker.*

I wrote "Meditation on the Golden Gate Bridge" while swimming in an indoor-outdoor pool at the Howard Johnson in Roanoke, Virginia, wondering why I could never love the poems of Charles Wright. The boy pianist-composer in the poem is Kit Armstrong, whose symphony "Celebration," composed at the age of seven, was premiered with the Pacific Symphony Orchestra.

"To Step in God's Cloud" was partially written in collaboration with Mary Leader. It is an acrostic.

In "Hope, prosthesis for," it should be noted that Nietzsche had an average-sized penis for his time.

Three-fourths of "Plagiarism" is borrowed from *The Gospel Worker's Treasury of Hymn and Revival Anecdotes, Texts, Subjects, Outlines, and Scripture Readings,* compiled by Rev. E. S. Lorenz, published by W. J. Shuey, 1887.

In "A Brief History of Patriotism," the statistics and language about potato consumption are taken from the Food and Agriculture Organization of the United Nations (*FAO Production*, Vol. 48, Rome, 1995).

"A Few Inches of Dead Flesh" is for, not about, Mary Leader.

"Suicide Poem" is for the poet who wrote *Long Distance* and *Inflorescence*.

The boy alluded to at the beginning of "Adorno" is not Adorno.

"Estimada Sra. Dear Abby:" was translated by Steven J. Stewart.

In 13th-century France, the fabliau was a comic form that involved innumerable cunts (and/or pricks). In 21st-century America, however, I have had to replace a cunt with a vagina in my poem, because a cunt can no longer be so named.

"Green Zone New Orleans" was first performed on April 26, 2007, at the Nomad Bookhouse in Jackson, Michigan.

The epigraph for "September 12" is a bastardization of Wittgenstein's first proposition in *Tractatus Logico-Philosophicus*: "The world is all that is the case."

On some level, "Last Flight Out of a State of Mind" is about United Airlines Flight 93.

In "Firefighter Song," the line "Time would not always be ours" is a modification of Ben Jonson's line "Time will not be ours forever."

"Funeral Direction" is a kind of inversion of Susan Stewart's "The Seasons."

ACKNOWLEDGMENTS

Grateful acknowledgment is made to the following magazines where some of these poems first appeared, sometimes in altered states: *Blackbird, The Canary, Conduit, Court Green, Del Sol Review, Denver Quarterly, elimae, Exile Quarterly, Green Mountains Review, Gulf Coast, Jacket, LIT, The New Yinzer, Octopus, The Pinch, Practice, Quick Fiction, RealPoetik, River City, Sentence, Smartish Pace, So to Speak, Studio, Third Coast,* and *Zyzzyva.*

Thank you to Paul Slovak, my editor at Penguin; to Ray Caesar for his cover art; and to Central Michigan University for an alternative assignment.

Thank you to Annie Goldman for her constant and immeasurable love, patience, and support, especially during my summer vacation.

ABOUT THE AUTHOR

Mark Yakich lives in New Orleans.

PENGUIN POETS

JOHN ASHBERY
Selected Poems
*Self-Portrait in a Convex
  Mirror*

TED BERRIGAN
The Sonnets

PHILIP BOOTH
Selves

JIM CARROLL
*Fear of Dreaming:
  The Selected Poems*
Living at the Movies
Void of Course

ALISON HAWTHORNE
DEMING
Genius Loci

CARL DENNIS
*New and Selected Poems
  1974–2004*
Practical Gods
Ranking the Wishes
Unknown Friends

DIANE DI PRIMA
Loba

STUART DISCHELL
Backwards Days
Dig Safe

STEPHEN DOBYNS
Mystery, So Long
*Pallbearers Envying the
  One Who Rides*
The Porcupine's Kisses
*Velocities: New and Selected
  Poems: 1966–1992*

EDWARD DORN
*Way More West: New and
  Selected Poems*

ROGER FANNING
Homesick

AMY GERSTLER
Crown of Weeds
Ghost Girl
Medicine
Nerve Storm

EUGENE GLORIA
*Drivers at the Short-Time
  Motel*
Hoodlum Birds

DEBORA GREGER
*Desert Fathers, Uranium
  Daughters*
God
Western Art

TERRANCE HAYES
Hip Logic
Wind in a Box

ROBERT HUNTER
*A Box of Rain: Lyrics:
  1965–1993*
Sentinel and Other Poems

MARY KARR
Viper Rum

JACK KEROUAC
Book of Blues
Book of Haikus
Book of Sketches

JOANNA KLINK
Circadian

ANN LAUTERBACH
Hum
*If in Time: Selected Poems,
  1975–2000*
On a Stair

CORINNE LEE
PYX

PHILLIS LEVIN
May Day
Mercury

WILLIAM LOGAN
Macbeth in Venice
Night Battle
Vain Empires
The Whispering Gallery

MICHAEL MCCLURE
*Huge Dreams: San Francisco
  and Beat Poems*

DAVID MELTZER
*David's Copy: The Selected
  Poems of David Meltzer*

CAROL MUSKE
An Octave Above Thunder
Red Trousseau

ALICE NOTLEY
Disobedience
In the Pines
Mysteries of Small Houses

LAWRENCE RAAB
The Probable World
*Visible Signs: New and
  Selected Poems*

BARBARA RAS
One Hidden Stuff

PATTIANN ROGERS
Generations

WILLIAM STOBB
Nervous Systems

STEPHANIE STRICKLAND
*V: WaveSon.nets/Losing
  L'una*

TRYFON TOLIDES
*An Almost Pure Empty
  Walking*

ANNE WALDMAN
Kill or Cure
Marriage: A Sentence
*Structure of the World
  Compared to a Bubble*

JAMES WELCH
Riding the Earthboy 40

PHILIP WHALEN
Overtime: Selected Poems

ROBERT WRIGLEY
*Earthly Meditations: New
  and Selected Poems*
Lives of the Animals
Reign of Snakes

MARK YAKICH
*The Importance of Peeling
  Potatoes in Ukraine*
*Unrelated Individuals
  Forming a Group Waiting
  to Cross*

JOHN YAU
Borrowed Love Poems
Paradiso Diaspora

Printed in the United States
by Baker & Taylor Publisher Services